Coping With ...
A Guidebook ...

Copyright © 2020 POOLSON | ODEN

All rights reserved. No part of this book may be reproduced or transmitted in any form or by any means without written permission from the authors.

One Lakeway
3900 N. Causeway Blvd.
Suite 680
Metairie, LA 70002
(504) 766-2200 | Office
(833) 505-2122 | Toll Free

WWW.POOLSONODEN.COM

TABLE OF CONTENTS

What to Expect After Your Husband's Injury — 7
- Your Husband Will be Asked to Give a Statement — 7
- He Will be Encouraged to See a Company Doctor — 9
- He Will Receive Advice From Everyone — 10

What Can You Do to Help Your Husband? — 13
- Photograph His Injury and Any Surgeries — 13
- Save Emails and Paperwork — 14
- Be Involved in Your Husband's Medical Care — 15
- Apply for Short-Term and Long-Term Disability — 17
- Railroad Unemployment and Sickness Benefits — 19
- Help Him Find Legal Counsel if Necessary — 24
- Encourage Him NOT to Use Social Media — 25

Frequently Asked Questions — 27
- Does the Company Have to Keep Him Employed? — 27
- Should He Return to Work as Soon as Possible? — 28
- Will They Try to Videotape Him After His Injury? — 33
- Is the Railroad Your Husband's Friend? — 35

FAQs About Filing a Claim — 38
- How Much Will My Husband's Case be Worth? — 38
- Must a Claim be Filed Before Seeking Treatment? — 39
- How Long Will Your Husband's Claim Take? — 41
- Do You Have a Personal Claim as a Spouse? — 42

Think Long-Term, Not Short-Term	43
Short-Term Fixes with Long-Term Problems	44
Returning to Work Too Quickly	44
Giving a Recorded Statement	44
Seeking Medical Treatment Through the Company	45
How to Think Long-Term	47
Your Husband's Physical & Emotional Journey	49
His Shrinking Social Circle	49
He May be Hurting More Than He Lets On	50
Frustration About the Future	51
Being on the Same Page	52
Emotional Support You Can Offer	53
Giving Him Hope	53
Seeing the Positives of a Career Change	55
Letting Him Know You Support Him	56
Coming to Terms with Filing a Claim	57
Changes at Home	61
Ideas to Help Your Husband Cope at Home	64
Appreciating the Extra Time with Family	64
Give Him Some Responsibilities	66
Help Him Associate with Non-Railroad Friends	69
Help Him Find Spiritual/Religious Guidance	69
Life After Filing a Claim	70
Use Settlement Money Wisely	70
Living Without Regret and What-Ifs	71
**About Us & POOLSON	ODEN Law Firm**	73

DISCLAIMER:

This book is meant for informational purposes only. The legal statutes mentioned in this book were current as of the publication date, however, we cannot guarantee that these statutes have remained the same since the publication date. The information contained herein is not intended, and should not be taken, as legal advice. You are advised to contact a railroad attorney for counsel on particular issues and concerns. Additionally, your use or request of our materials does not constitute as an attorney-client relationship between you and POOLSON | ODEN Law Firm.

"We can't always control what happens to us, only our response. And it is in this response that we find empowerment, strength, inspiration, and our opportunity."

Your First Step

You are about to walk the same road traveled by hundreds of wives of railroad workers whose husbands suffered injuries while working for the railroad, either on the road or in the yard. These women have faced many challenges, and our office has had the real honor of helping many of these women through this tough time. We like to think we contributed in great part to a better future for them, their husbands, and their families.

This guidebook is meant to address many of the common issues that arise after your husband suffers an injury while working for the railroad. Some of the advice you may find helpful, some may scare you, while some will simply upset you. We know you didn't ask to be in the position you now find yourself, just like your husband didn't ask to be hurt doing a job he loved to support his family. And a question you might be asking yourself is "Why is this happening to us?"

While you may not be able to change what happened to you and your family, you CAN change what WILL happen. Only understanding your situation, what he is going through and what you can do to help him will move you both forward to a better place. This guide is the first step in doing so.

Danny Poolson & Carisa Oden
POOLSON | ODEN Law Firm

What to Expect After Your Husband's Injury

Your Husband Will Be Asked To Give A Statement

If he didn't already give one immediately after his accident, your husband may discuss this with you and whether or not he should give a statement to railroad management.

Unfortunately, most companies take recorded statements for a very specific reason: to have your husband say on record that the company did not do anything wrong to cause or contribute to his injury.

They do this so they can protect themselves if your husband ends up filing a claim. We'll discuss the option of filing a claim later in the book, but to put it briefly, how much money the company pays to your husband for his injury is related to whether or not the company was at fault for causing his injury.

If your husband chooses to give a recorded statement, be sure to encourage him to be fully honest and explain everything that happened, including anything the company did (or did not do) to cause his accident.

If the railroad didn't maintain equipment properly, or did not provide proper tools, then that's something that should be noted in the statement. Any unsafe condition should be noted in the statement. This is a very stressful situation for your husband, especially if he has worked for his company for a long period of time. He may be worried for his job or what may happen. Your husband will be extremely reluctant to blame coworkers for anything they did wrong in connection with his accident.

We encourage you to discuss this at length with him so that he understands he shouldn't accept full blame for the accident if that wasn't the case.

Accepting full blame for the accident, or failing to point out what could have been done to avoid the accident, will potentially hurt him down the road.

He Will Be Encouraged To See A Company Doctor

Your husband's railroad typically will want to control his medical treatment and tell him he can only see physicians that they select.

They do this for several reasons: (1) it keeps your husband dependent on the company, (2) it allows them to monitor his medical treatment (or lack thereof), (3) it prevents your husband from getting MRIs, CT scans, or other expensive and necessary tests, etc., which may reveal the seriousness of his injury, (4) it's cheaper because they're not paying an outside doctor to run expensive tests, and (5) their doctor can say he's "fully recovered" and send him back to work before he's ready (this ties into the legal side which we will explain later).

We encourage you and him to seek treatment from your own trusted physician who will give you the necessary tests you need to discover the extent of the injury. The important thing to remember is that you should be on alert for the railroad not giving your husband the full medical treatment he needs to get better.

He Will Receive Advice From Everyone

It is important to recognize that much of this advice will be conflicting advice. We always encourage our clients to educate themselves fully about all of their options, meet with their trusted family members, make a firm decision on the manner in which to proceed, and then move forward from that point without looking back.

Your husband will go crazy if he compares advice from one individual to the next since each person will have a different opinion about what he should do. Again, we recommend you help him obtain as much information as possible about all of his options and then, as a family unit, make an informed decision as to how best to proceed without looking back.

During the first few weeks of your husband's injury understand that he will have a real uncertainty about his future and about what he should do on a daily basis. Your husband will be facing one of the most uncertain times of his life following his injury. It is important that you are aware of this and try to give him as much support as possible. The next chapter discusses some of the ways you can lend your support.

Don't Get Railroaded™
Railroaders' Steps After An On-duty Injury

The minute an injury happens, the Railroad circles the wagons and puts your husband on the other side of the tracks. Their goal is to control the evidence and the story of what happened to blame your husband. Help your husband use the following steps to protect you and your family:

1. GET MEDICAL ATTENTION
Take an ambulance if needed or get to your own doctor ASAP - Don't wait!

2. GIVE COMPLETE & ACCURATE HISTORY TO DOCTORS
Make sure he gives details of each body part that hurts and exactly how the accident happened.

3. DON'T BE PRESSURED TO LET RAILROAD MANAGERS TALK TO YOUR HUSBAND'S DOCTORS
Just because the Railroad pays the bills does not mean that management can talk to your doctor. Simply tell your doctor you do not want management in the examining room.

4. FILL OUT THE PERSONAL INJURY REPORT AS SOON AS POSSIBLE
Most carriers have a rule that the report must be filled out as soon as possible. Fill out as soon as your husband feels capable and do not let management fill out for your husband to sign. Always list ALL parts of his body that hurt and any defective conditions/equipment which caused his accident.

5. APPLY FOR RRB SICKNESS BENEFITS AND DISABILITY BENEFITS
It takes time for these benefits to start and his doctors will need to fill out forms if your husband is going to be out longer than 30 days, so apply sooner rather than later.

6. DO NOT GIVE A RECORDED STATEMENT TO CLAIMS DEPARTMENT
Your husband is NOT legally required to give a statement and it benefits no one but the Railroad.

7. WRITE DOWN DETAILS OF THE ACCIDENT
Get names and phone numbers of any witnesses and co-workers to your husband's accident. When he gets home, have him write down all the details in a notebook while it is fresh in his mind.

POOLSON | ODEN
RAILROAD INJURY ATTORNEYS
Copyright © 2019, Poolson Oden

Don't Get Left Alone On The Wrong Side Of The Tracks.
Toll Free | (833) 505-2122

What Can You Do to Help Your Husband?

Here is a brief listing of specific action items that you can do to help your husband. These items will help him deal with the financial, emotional, and possible legal difficulty both you and he may face following his injury.

Photograph His Injury and Any Surgeries

If at some point you decide to hire an attorney and pursue a case, you will want to have photographs of the injury. Even if you don't file a claim, it may be wise to document the injury if you have to prove to the railroad that he's actually hurt. It is important for him to take photographs of his injury and any type of surgeries which he may have in the future following his injury. Photographs of bruising and swelling can be important down the road in order to show the serious nature of his injury. Photographs of surgeries and surgical scars are important to show what he has been through. You want to remind your husband that weeks and months after an injury occurs it is often very difficult to fully show the seriousness of what he had been through.

Save Emails and Paperwork

Remind your husband to save emails and documents which in any way relate to his employment and/or accident. Often there are emails and texts sent back and forth immediately following an accident and injury. If they are on a company-based email server, you can forward them to your private email address as a way of saving them. If possible, you should also print out a copy of these and save them in a safe location. Your husband may also have documents which are important to his accident and injury as well as his employment with his company. We encourage you to obtain a folder to keep all of these documents in so that they may be used at a later date if necessary. Like the pictures, it is important to save documentation relating to the injury. You never know when you might need it.

Be Involved in Your Husband's Medical Care

Your husband will be attending many doctor appointments following his railroad injury. We encourage you to attend all of these appointments with him if possible. This is important for several reasons. First, it will give him moral support and make it easier for him to attend these appointments. There is nothing more frustrating and isolating than sitting in a doctor's office by yourself wondering if you should be at the appointment or not. It is helpful for you to be there with him for support.

The railroad can't make an employee see a company doctor. You husband may take the "recommendations" of his supervisor or manager and see this doctor to not rock the boat or make his boss angry. Your husband can see whatever doctor he chooses – the railroad cannot force him to see a company doctor. If he sees the recommended doctor, it is important for you to be in the room.

Routinely our clients will advise us that the company-chosen physician verbally told them something during the evaluation which ends up being very different than what the physician puts in his written report. If you are present during the appointment, you will be able to keep the company-chosen doctor honest and your husband safe from mistreatment.

Another extremely important reason for you to attend your husband's doctor appointments is to help him fill out all of the paperwork correctly. You know how men are with paperwork! Very often there will be questionnaire forms provided to your husband during his doctor appointments. These forms often ask how his injury occurred and whether it was work-related or not.

It may be difficult for your husband to honestly explain on the form what happened and who was potentially at fault. In his mind, it may seem easier to quickly write only half the story. This could be a problem if later the railroad uses this paperwork as evidence that your husband wasn't injured or didn't think the railroad was to blame. It is important for you to be there to encourage him to be honest on the form and to correctly document how his injury occurred at work.

Apply for Short-Term and Long-Term Disability

If your husband has short-term or long-term disability through work, we suggest you help him apply for these benefits. It could be an alternate source of income during this financially uncertain time. Be aware that your husband's railroad may discourage him from applying for short-term or long-term disability. Often the railroad will tell him that because his injury happened at work it is not "covered" under short-term or long-term disability. We encourage all injured railroad workers to apply for short-term and long- term disability regardless of whether or not their companies believe the injury will be covered. The worst that can happen is he will simply be denied.

You should also understand that his railroad has very little interest in seeing that he obtains short-term or long- term disability while he is injured. If your husband is able to successfully obtain his disability benefits, he will be much less dependent upon the railroad for his other advances that the railroad may be paying to him. In short, his railroad will lose its ability to control him and his future if he is able to obtain disability benefits.

Railroad Unemployment and Sickness Benefits

The Railroad Retirement Board ("RRB") provides benefits to railroad employees to restore their lost wages when they have period of unemployment or sickness. These benefits are based on biweekly claims that are filed with the RRB, and certain funds are paid directly to railroad workers for unemployment or for sickness. The benefit year for any of these benefits of unemployment or sickness begins July 1.

In order for a railroader to qualify, your husband must have earnings of at least $3,900.00 in any calendar year. If he does not meet those requirements, but has at least 10 years of service, he may still be able to qualify based on certain conditions.

It is important for your husband to apply for sickness benefits as soon as possible after an injury. Although he has to wait four (4) consecutive days of sickness or injury before the benefits will begin, it is important to start that process as quickly as possible because his physician who has seen him for his injury will have forms that are required to be filled out by the RRB. Your husband's doctor will need to complete the statement of sickness, which is part of the application.

Right now, the maximum daily benefit rate for sickness benefits is $78.00 per day. That daily rate will rise to $80.00 in July, 2020. You can obtain an application for sickness benefits on our website, www.poolsonoden.com. Your husband's union should also have a sickness benefit form. The form number is Form SSI-1A. Please contact our office for any help filling out the form, or explaining the form, and how the benefits work.

Once these forms are completed, you must mail them to the Railroad Retirement Board's (RRB) headquarters in Chicago within ten (10) days from when your husband becomes sick or injured. Once the RRB receives these forms, they will process the application and determine if your husband is eligible for sickness benefits. Once the RRB processes the application, it will provide your husband with biweekly claims, which will be made available online, and they will be mailed to your husband.

If your husband receives sickness benefits and has a claim or lawsuit against the railroad where he recovers monies either through a verdict or settling of his personal injury claim, the RRB has a right of recovery for those benefits. Meaning, if your husband recovers money from a lawsuit or claim, the RRB can seek to recover those benefits previously paid. Those benefits will be paid back from any proceeds your husband receives in settlement.

In addition to sickness benefits, railroaders with certain months of service may also be eligible for a disability annuity or a total disability. If your husband has 240 months of service, which is the equivalent of 20 years, and he is unable to perform his regular railroading job, he may qualify for what the Railroad Retirement Board calls an "occupational disability" or an "occupational annuity." He will have to submit an application that details all of his medical history from his physicians that supports his claim that he is not able to perform his railroading job.

On the other hand, a total disability is available if, after your husband has been in railroad service for 120 months or 10 years, he has a permanent condition that does not allow him to perform any substantial gainful employment. This means that, in addition to his railroading job, your husband would not be able to do any other job that he could make money doing.

As an aside, many railroaders have experienced a time in their careers when they have been furloughed and unable to work. For instance, many

Railroaders were furloughed during the Covid-19 Pandemic. If your husband is furloughed, then there are unemployment benefits that he may be eligible for. Please contact our office with any questions about unemployment benefits and if your husband would be eligible for those benefits as well.

For more information about Railroad Retirement Board disability annuities or total disability annuities, the Railroad Retirement Board's website has a wealth of information.

> U.S. Railroad Retirement Board
> William O. Lipinski Federal Building
> 844 North Rush Street
> Chicago, IL 60611-1275
> Toll Free: (877) 772-5772
> TTY: (312) 751-4701
> Directory: (312) 751-4300
> https://www.rrb.gov/

You can always contact our office for more information and questions about these differences and nuances of railroading benefits.

Help Him Find Legal Counsel if Necessary

When we interview potential clients, one of our standard questions is whether or not the potential client is married. If so, we encourage him to bring his wife to our initial meeting so that she can take an active role in helping with and handling his case. If your husband meets with attorneys on his own, he will no doubt come home with questions as to whether he should hire the attorneys he just met with and whether or not he trusts the attorneys.

There's no way that you can participate in this conversation with him unless you were actually there meeting the attorneys and asking questions. In short, your husband's claim is one of the most important things that he will go through and thus it is one of the most important things you will go through as his spouse. We encourage you to get involved in deciding which attorney is best to handle your husband's case if you two decide to pursue one.

Encourage Him NOT to Use Social Media

Today most workers are engaged in some type of social media through Facebook, Twitter, or LinkedIn. It is important for your husband to avoid discussing his accident and injury on social media sites. It is now the law that Facebook pages, LinkedIn pages, and other websites can potentially be used against him during a case.

Remind your husband of this and make sure he is not posting information about his accident or injury online. He should also avoid discussing his recreational, physical, or family activities online. We encourage all of our clients to simply stop using social media during a case.

How You Can Help Your Husband After A Railroad Injury

1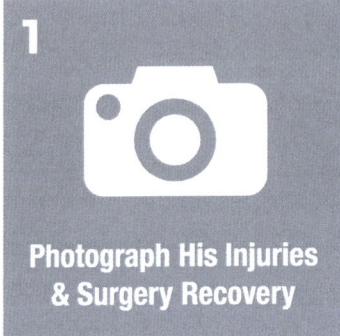
Photograph His Injuries & Surgery Recovery

2
Save Emails & Paperwork

3
Be Involved In His Medical Care

4
Apply For Short & Long-Term Disability

5
Find Legal Counsel If Necessary

6
Refrain From Facebook & Other Social Media

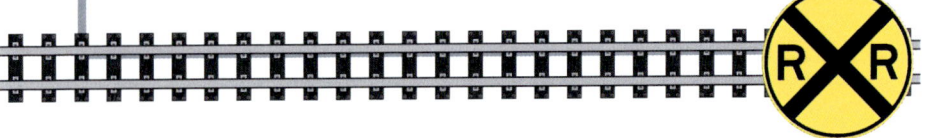

Frequently Asked Questions

As a spouse of an injured railroad worker, you will have many questions that you would like answered following your husband's on-duty injury. Here is a list of questions that many of our clients have struggled with.

Does the Railroad Have to Keep Him Employed?

Yes. The railroad cannot fire a railroader for simply having an injury. However, many Railroads charge employees with rule violations in connection with the accident or charge a worker for not timely reporting an injury. To combat this retaliation, all railroad workers are protected by the Federal Railroad Safety Act (FRSA), which was enacted to promote safety in all areas of railroad operations and to ensure that railroad employees engaging in certain protected activities under the Act could do so without the fear or threat of discrimination or retaliation from their railroad employer. Under federal law, the railroad is not allowed to fire, harass, or intimidate your husband in connection with reporting an injury.

Your husband should be aware of his railroad's rules, under which he may have an obligation to report all injuries promptly.

Should He Return to Work as Soon as Possible?

There are several reasons why it may not be in his best interest to return to work as quickly as possible.

The first and most important reason is that **returning to work too soon could worsen the injury, cause a new injury, and/or prevent full recovery.** If your child was sick or injured, you wouldn't let him/her go outside and play until you knew that he/she was 100% better.

And while your spouse may be under pressure from the railroad and from his need to provide for you and the family, it is important to consider the long-term implications if he returns to work too soon before he has healed completely: he may make his injury worse and make it harder to recover fully. If his injury worsens, he'll have more medical problems, more doctor's visits, more medical bills and expenses.

The second reason why it'd be a bad idea to return to work too soon has to do with filing a case. If you were to file a claim, it is important for you to understand how the compensation process works because this is going to determine how much money the railroad will pay your spouse for his injury.

In all likelihood your husband was making excellent money working for the railroad. In almost all railroad injury cases a very significant portion of any damages (compensation) relates directly to the loss of future wages due to your husband's inability to return to work for the railroad. For example if your husband is 40 years old and is earning approximately $80,000.00 per year working as a railroader, and he then suffers an injury which prevents him from returning to work and only makes $20,000.00 per year in some other job, he's losing $60,000.00 per year. When this yearly loss is calculated over 10 or 20 years, it can easily add up to hundreds of thousands of dollars in potential compensation.

The only way to prove that your husband deserves this large amount of money is to prove that he is unable to go back to work full-time. If your husband attempts to return to work as quickly as possible and is successful at enduring work for a few weeks or months, he has essentially proven that he is able to return to full-duty work earning the same amount of pay he was earning before his accident and injury.

Even though he is in pain the whole time and barely able to perform his tasks, he has shown on the record that he can work. The railroad would then use this as evidence later to say that he doesn't deserve the compensation of lost wages. We routinely counsel that injured workers should return to work if, and only if, they are completely certain that they are fully capable of returning to 100 percent unrestricted very heavy manual labor.

In such a situation, the individual is fully capable of returning to unlimited, unrestricted work and thus he actually can earn as much money as he used to earn whether it for his current employer or another employer down the road.

Unfortunately, in the vast majority of cases, clients have not recovered 100 percent from their injuries and they are forced by their employers to return to work railroading before they are ready.

In these cases, we strongly caution that they should not return to work as this is simply a tactic used by their employer to ruin any type of future claim that they may have for loss of wages. (**Read that last sentence again please—it is extremely important.)

Your husband's railroad knows the law and fully understands that the sooner it can have him return to full duty unlimited work, the more likely it is they have avoided a claim for hundreds of thousands of dollars or more in loss of future wages. It is critical to understand this so that you may then best determine whether or not your husband should return to work as soon as possible following his injury.

Finally, all railroads will require a worker to obtain a full-duty release before they will allow him to return to work following his injury. So essentially if your husband thinks he will "attempt" to return to work on a trial period and see if he can do it, this is simply not realistic. Instead, he will be required to obtain a full-duty release from his physician and this may then prevent him from claiming any type of lost wages down the road. It may also prevent him from obtaining further medical treatment if his condition worsens after he attempts to return to work.

Will They Try to Videotape Him After His Injury?

This is one of the most unfortunate aspects of your husband's railroad injury. While he may have been a tremendous asset to his company before his accident and injury, he is now viewed as an "open claim" within the company.

In this regard the railroad will typically try to videotape him after his injury in order to obtain evidence to use against him. This does not mean that he needs to hide inside 24 hours a day.

Rather, as we advise our clients, he should simply act consistently in his daily activities as he is indicating to his physicians. You should, however, be aware of situations in which he tries to "push" himself or more likely, situations where he becomes frustrated and tired of living with daily restrictions on his activities.

In the past we have seen our railroad clients attempt to hunt or fish with their friends even though their injury makes it very difficult. We have also seen our clients try to go four- wheel riding as a social activity even though they are in pain and it is difficult for them to do with their injury.

Be aware if your husband begins to ignore his limitations simply because he is frustrated or tired of dealing with his injury. You should try to counsel him that it is best for him not to push himself and he should avoid strenuous-type activities no matter how frustrated he is with his situation.

Is the Railroad Your Husband's Friend?

This is a difficult question to answer because many of our clients simply do not want to hear the answer. In general, once an on-duty injury occurs, the railroad plays a very different role and has a very different relationship with your husband than it did before his injury.

As we said before, once your husband is injured, he is a potential liability to the railroad. In their eyes, he could file a lawsuit against them at any moment, even if he has no intention to do so. Because they view him this way, they will immediately treat him differently.

To begin with, railroad injuries are often handled by individuals working in the office. Sometimes these individuals do not even work in the local office and instead are based out of some large corporate headquarters in a different city or state.

Your husband thinks of his "railroad" as all of his

wonderful coworkers that he worked with on the train or in the rail yard during his employment. In some cases, he may actually know these individuals from around his hometown area.

It is fundamental that you explain to him that these are not the individuals who will make any determinations in regard to keeping him employed in the future, payment of his claim, paying for his medical treatment, and ultimately any type of settlement which may be paid on his case.

We have found over the years that some of your husband's co-workers might actually encourage him to obtain an attorney and file a claim because they can see the writing on the wall before he does.

We would encourage your husband to distinguish between "the railroad" that he knew and loved while he worked for it prior to his injury and "the railroad" that is now handling his claim and is well aware of all of its, and your husband's, rights and the laws which apply to his injury.

THE COMPANY
Before & After A Railroad Injury

BEFORE

Views the worker as a valuable asset
The company is willing to invest in the worker in hopes of making more money.

Treats the Worker Like Family
The company in charge of the worker's day to day is embodied by the individuals on the railroad who know the worker personally.

Trusts the Worker
The company generally trusts the worker.

AFTER

Views the injured worker as a liability
The company will safeguard itself from the possible financial loss related to an injury lawsuit.

Treats the Worker Like a Stranger
The company responsible for the injured worker's medical treatment & financial well-being is comprised of individuals from the railroad who are impersonal and impartial to the worker.

Distrusts the Injured Worker
The company will videotape every action taken by the injured worker both on & off the clock.

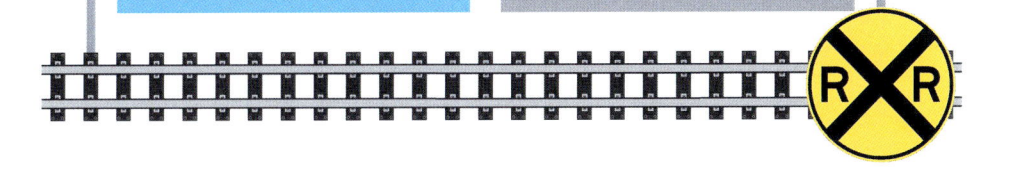

FAQs About Filing a Claim

How Much Will My Husband's Case be Worth?

Certainly every case must be evaluated on the facts of the case. There are a few basic, important factors, though, which generally determine the difference between a relatively small valued case and a higher valued case.

If he has suffered an injury which prevents him from returning to his railroad craft and he previously earned significant wages working for the railroad, in all likelihood he will have a significant loss of future wage claim. Most high dollar railroad injury claims involve significant loss of wage claims in addition to pain and suffering damages and medical expenses.

One way to estimate the value of your husband's railroad claim is to ask how much money he will earn returning to limited or light duty work following his railroad injury. More often than not, there is no light duty work available at the railroad. You will then need to compare this amount of income with what he was earning railroading. This begins to give you an idea of the amount of lost wages your husband may suffer due to his injury.

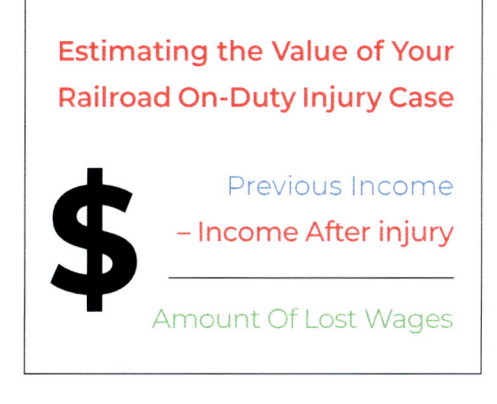

Estimating the Value of Your Railroad On-Duty Injury Case

$

Previous Income
− Income After injury
_____
Amount Of Lost Wages

Must a Claim be Filed Before Seeking Treatment?

No, your husband does not need to file a claim before seeking medical treatment. His first priority is always his health. If injured on the job, he should take care of his medical needs immediately; filing a FELA claim or other railroad claim post-treatment does not bar him from eligibility for benefits.

In fact, it doesn't make much sense to file a claim before seeking care because he has yet to discover the extent of his injury. Worry about legal matters after he's seen the doctor.

It's important to understand that railroaders are required to report their on-duty injuries and fill out a personal injury report for their railroad employer as soon as possible. However, your husband does not have to fill out a personal injury report until he is capable in body and mind. This means that if your husband is in shock, pain, in the hospital undergoing treatment, taking medications that could affect his ability to completely fill out the personal injury report, he can agree to fill out the report as soon as he is ready. Please see our *Personal Injury Form Checklist* to help fill out this vital report and contact your experienced FELA attorneys as soon as possible for advice.

While seeking treatment, your husband's railroad employer (through its health insurance company) is legally responsible for medical bills related to his injury.

How Long Will Your Husband's Claim Take?

If your husband chooses to pursue a claim in court, his claim will typically take approximately twelve (12) months to fifteen (15) months before it ends. This will vary from court to court but in general if his claim is filed in federal court, it typically takes approximately 12 - 15 months from beginning to end. While this may seem like a long time, it is important to understand that during this period, he is receiving needed medical treatment and his case will be progressing as statements and depositions will be taken from coworkers. Often experts are hired and they need to review materials and issue written reports during this time period.

The court will also set cutoff deadlines a few months before his actual trial date which means that his case will be prepared during the six to nine-month period after it is initially filed. If a settlement is reached in his case, the settlement is typically paid within thirty (30) days of the agreement. In the majority of the cases that we file for our clients in federal court, we find that they are resolved and receive their money within approximately twelve (12) months of filing suit.

If your husband's case goes to trial, this can delay collecting any type of judgment further into the future, however the length of delay depends in large part upon the court in which the case is tried.

Do You Have a Personal Claim as a Spouse?

If your husband is a railroader under the law, then unfortunately as his spouse you are not entitled to file any type of claim on your own seeking monetary damages. You have no right to collect any damages if he is a railroader. While the Federal Employers Liability Act ("FELA") is an excellent law that provides wonderful protection to your husband as an injured worker, the one unfortunate flaw of FELA is that it specifically prohibits spouses of injured railroaders from filing any type of claim or collecting damages arising out of their husband's injury. Over the years we have found this to be tragically unfair since many times spouses suffer almost as significantly as the injured worker in terms of emotional uncertainty about your future and helping and caring for your injured husband while he attempts to recover.

Think Long-Term, Not Short-Term

Following his on-duty railroad injury, your husband may be thinking "short-term". Your husband simply wants to fix what has happened, and he wants to do it as quickly as possible. Most often, however, a serious railroad injury needs a long-term solution.

We see many common examples of short-term efforts to quickly fix what has happened. All too often they cause more damage to the injured worker. These short-term fixes give him less options in the future, not more.

Short-Term Fixes with Long-Term Problems

Returning to Work Too Quickly

He will simply want to go back to earning the money that he earned before he was injured and in doing so, your husband may rush back to work too quickly before he is physically able to. This can worsen his injury and ruin any type of claim he may have down the road.

Giving a Recorded Statement to Keep Them Happy

He is doing this because he still associates himself with the railroad and he believes that if he in any way blames the railroad or his coworkers for his accident, that the railroad will then be upset with him for doing so. You should explain to him that the railroad is not going to be upset at him for telling the truth about the accident (or it should not be upset at him if it is truly just trying to investigate what happened).

Seeking Medical Treatment Through the Company

Simply seeing the company-chosen physicians instead of demanding that he be allowed to see his own trusted doctors can be devastating to both his injury and any potential future case. Be on alert for this type of short-term fix since his medical treatment is one of the most important aspects following his injury.

There are many reasons why your husband may be thinking short-term rather than long-term following his injury. These are not "bad" reasons nor do they mean he is doing anything intentionally wrong. We have represented railroad workers for more than twenty (20) years, combined, and the reason these individuals love railroading is because they are generally "fix it" type individuals. This means that they often want to immediately solve a problem as quickly as possible. This is the exact reason they enjoy railroading and why they are often excellent railroad workers and truly love their careers. However, after a serious railroad injury, unfortunately they simply do not have the knowledge or information required to make the best decisions in regard to how to "fix" what has happened.

We often tell our clients that if we were to work for the railroad, we would certainly rely upon them to show us the ropes and explain to us how things worked on the railroad. In a similar way, our railroad clients are often best served by relying upon trusted legal advice as to their rights and options. Your husband is now in the same situation and it will be very difficult for him to accept advice from anyone else.

How to Think Long-Term

One way you can help your husband think long-term rather than short-term is to ask the question "where will this get us in three years or more down the road?"

Each decision he makes following his railroad injury should pass this test. By way of example, if the railroad convinced him to see the railroad company doc rather than his own physician and he is only being provided with company-chosen medical treatment, this will not serve him long-term.

If he were truly concerned about his long-term health three years or more down the road, he would see his own trusted physician and insist that any and all possible medical testing be done to determine the full nature and extent of his injury.

Similarly, if he is asked to provide a tape-recorded statement, and he is thinking three years or more down the road, he will not withhold important information about the accident including actions that the railroad could have taken to avoid the accident.

Instead, he will realize that there is a high likelihood he may not be with the railroad three years down the road and it is more important to properly document all the ways that his accident could have been avoided rather than him simply keeping the railroad happy for another three weeks or three months.

Your Husband's Physical and Emotional Journey

In representing hundreds of injured railroad workers and their families over the years, we have seen what individuals go through emotionally and physically following an injury. If you understand what your husband may be going through, you can better help him deal with it.

His Shrinking Social Circle

Typically following a railroad injury, your husband will not be socializing as much with his company friends. While this may seem insignificant, it can often be difficult for your husband's social circles to change following his injury. So understand that he might start feeling restless or lonely from not seeing his former friends as often.

He May be Hurting More Than He Lets On

Your husband will be dealing with physical pain and discomfort associated with his injury. While this may seem obvious and at this stage you are probably well aware of his physical suffering, it is helpful to remember that he did not choose to put himself in the situation that he is in.

Often railroad workers will internalize a lot of their pain and discomfort. Unfortunately, this means that they can be difficult to deal with following their injuries. Try to recognize that hopefully this very difficult time will not be permanent and it is something that you all will weather together.

Frustration About the Future

Finally, one very emotional aspect of your husband's accident and injury is the fact that he is facing a lot of uncertainty about his future. Again, you are also going through this with him.

However, most railroad workers pride themselves on being "can do" type individuals. Many of our clients have never had to relinquish control of their future to anything or anyone. Railroad workers are generally self-starters who take action quickly. (This is one of the many, many reasons we love helping railroaders and their families.)

If your husband has suffered any type of serious railroad injury, then he is now prevented from doing all of this. In short, a lot of his emotional stress will come from having little to no control over his short-term future and having great uncertainty as to his long-term future. Simply by recognizing this and being aware of it will help you support him over the next few months.

Being on the Same Page

You should realize that taking action is very hard and your husband needs your support in regard to any decisions he makes following his injury. One of the hardest things our clients have to do is file a claim against the railroad that they viewed as the way to fully provide for their families. Roadroaders universally love what they do and take pride in their crafts.

Unfortunately, some of our clients and their spouses do not agree with each other in regard to whether or not a claim should be filed. We have seen some spouses who are less than 100 percent supportive of their husband filing a claim. We surmise that these spouses may have been more worried about short-term financial issues and "keeping the lights on" than about long-term stability of their husband and families.

This is certainly understandable, but it is not the best long-term approach. Whenever possible we encourage husbands and spouses to be 100 percent on the same page in terms of pursuing a railroad injury claim.

Emotional Support You Can Offer

Giving Him Hope: The Idea of Returning to Work

One way you can encourage him is to tell him he may still be able to return to railroading down the road after his injury has healed.

Even if he decides to file a claim, he can still return to work after the claim is resolved. He will very likely disagree with this statement and argue that once a claim is filed he will be "blacklisted" or "blackballed" with a target on his back.

The truth is that railroad cannot stop your husband from trying to return to his former position after his doctors have cleared him to return to work. Many of our clients have successfully returned to work after they healed.

Whether or not he can successfully return to railroading following an injury and/or a settlement will depend upon whether he physically can perform the work. This may depend upon him attending rehab until he has healed completely. During this time, he can pursue a claim, resolve the claim, and then ultimately return to railroad work.

Helping Him See the Positives of a Career Change

Next, you should encourage your husband that railroad work is not his only career option. This will be a very difficult discussion to have with your husband since he in all likelihood loved working on the railroad and he simply cannot see himself doing any other type of work at this time. Also, he will likely focus on the high wages that he earned railroading and insist that he will "never" make as much money working in another field.

While it is true that it could take a few years for him to progress in another career, there are other options for him following his injury.

We routinely have our clients meet with a vocational rehabilitation expert (a fancy title for a job expert) in order to identify and locate possible jobs for them following their railroad injuries. It is amazing what a year or two of additional training can accomplish to retrain an individual for a better paying career.

And the benefits of him working in a different career versus railroading go without saying (but we'll say it anyway): more time with you and the family, safer working conditions, more consistent schedule, more home-life support for you, among other benefits.

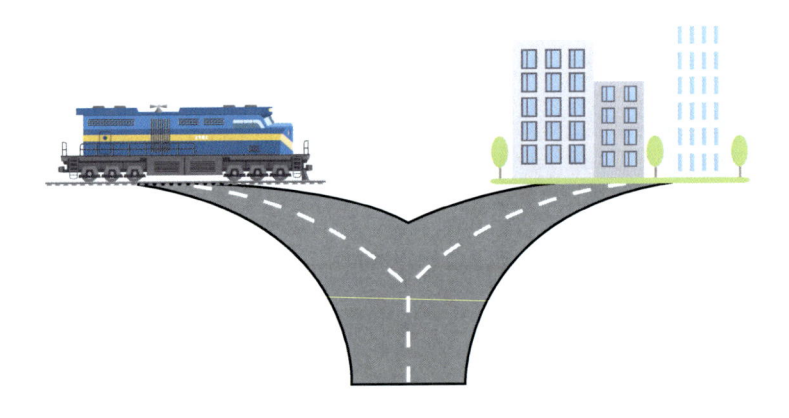

Letting Him Know You Support Him

We would encourage you to let your husband know that you and the kids are with him regardless of what type of work he does. As much as he may have associated himself with his railroad career before his injury, you should encourage him that his real life is at home with you and the family and his friends. His railroad job did not define him as much as he may have thought it did.

Helping Him Come to Terms with Filing a Claim

"We're not the suing type". That's what some of our nicest and most injured clients have said to us during our very first meetings with them. Deciding to file a claim is a very difficult decision. But sometimes cases simply have to be filed in court. You are not trying to attack the company, you are simply asking the railroad to take responsibility for the damage they have caused. That's all a claim is about. Very good people simply have to file claims in court when their rights are violated and a person has suffered a serious injury.

Many unlucky individuals are often left with no

choice but to pursue legal action in order to resolve a dispute with another. The legal system was designed for people who are being treated unjustly, individuals like a stay at home mom fighting her abusive husband for custody.

You would never think less of a woman who petitions the court to protect her children, nor will anyone think less of you or your husband if you must file a claim in court. His future and your future are simply too important to leave to chance.

When open and earnest communication fails and troubles go unresolved, sometimes the last option is to present your side of the story to an unbiased third party who can make a decision and help everyone move on.

This is frequently true of railroad workers who have been injured and need the railroad to provide for them financially. When the railroad fails to do so or fails to give enough to help you and your husband put your lives back together, this is when it becomes necessary to hire an attorney to help your husband present his case.

If you and your husband have decided to file a claim, encourage him that sometimes very good people simply have to file claims. Many in his same situation often feel tremendously guilty when they file a claim against a company that they have worked for. Your husband likely viewed his company as his "railroad family". They even refer to each other like that while they work on the railroad!

We explain to our clients that sometimes it is simply necessary to file a claim in court in order for us to explain the serious nature of the injury and the amount of money necessary for your family to live a normal life. You can imagine how hard it is for him to come to terms with the fact that it may be best for him (and his and your future financial stability) to file a claim against the railroad.

Many of our clients consider it this way, though. Your husband's company will only have to pay what the judge or jury believes it is responsible for. If the railroad did everything by the books and like they were supposed to, then that will emerge during the legal process. They'll prove they did everything they could to create a safe work environment and that his accident wasn't their fault.

But sometimes railroads will cut corners, skip safety procedures, and rush projects. This, too, will come out during the legal process and at that point the judge or jury will determine if the railroad could've done something different to prevent this tragedy from happening. Then they'll be required to pay the fair amount that your husband is entitled to under the law.

So, if the system is designed to only require the railroad to pay what it's responsible for, why should he feel any bit of guilt, shame, or hesitation to ask the company to take responsibility for their part in his accident?

Changes At Home

This idea deserves its own section because it is so important. In representing injured railroad workers for more than twenty (20) years, combined, one of the first realizations we had was that many railroad husbands and wives normally spend only half the year together.

Once a railroad injury occurs and your husband no longer goes to work on the railroad on a regular basis, you and he will be spending 100 percent of your time together.

For many couples this is a true blessing and they enjoy a relationship that existed when they first dated many years earlier.

However, for other couples this can be a real struggle. It can often be more difficult if you and your husband have a family together since he will now be spending additional time around the children. Again, while this can be a blessing in so many ways, it can also be a challenge.

Perhaps the best way to deal with the additional time that you will be spending together is to simply recognize it and understand that it will not be permanent. Even though your husband may be seriously injured and unable to obtain any type of regular employment at this time, he will certainly return to some form of work down the road. Even if his injury requires months or years of recovery, he will not be permanently staying at home every day for the rest of his life! At some point in time your lives will return to a more regular schedule.

There is a wonderful self-development speaker named Jim Rohn who has a philosophy that when you are in a relationship, you are 100 percent responsible for the success of that relationship. He believes that if each individual in the relationship has that attitude, there is no way the relationship can fail.

This is a hard philosophy to accept as most people feel that they are only 50 percent responsible for the success of any relationship, with the other individual also being 50 percent responsible. Jim Rohn disagrees. He encourages people to view themselves as being 100 percent responsible for the success of any relationship that they are in.

This might be an interesting discussion to have with your husband and it could be helpful to try this approach during the challenging months that you and he may face together after his railroad injury.

Ideas to Help Your Husband Cope at Home

Here are a few ideas on how you can help your husband cope at home after his railroad injury. These address emotional and financial issues that he, as well as you and your family, may be struggling with following his injury.

Help Him Appreciate the Extra Time with Family

We want to tell you a brief story about a recent client that we represented who was a young 30-something railroader who seriously injured his lower back at work. While his wife was working, he met with us during an initial consultation.

He was a wonderful individual and he had worked for several years for a short line railroad. He was earning more than $50,000.00 and he looked forward to many, many years of excellent income as a railroader. He had his whole career planned out.

He and his wife had been together for a few years and they had a young son. So, he was completely devastated after he had gotten hurt at work. All he kept repeating was that his career was over and that he had worked so hard to get where he was.

He had been extremely agitated and distraught during the first few months of his case. To say the least, he was very restless at home during the first few weeks after his injury. But during the course of his case, he confided in us that it had been a blessing in disguise. It had allowed him to spend critical months at home with his young son.

The point of this story is to simply focus on the blessing that you may have at home and encourage your husband to do the same.

Often railroad workers miss out on significant family moments and while your husband may not immediately recognize the extra time that he will have to spend with you and his children or family, you should be aware of this and try to encourage him to become more involved and active in their lives now that he is able to do so. If you and your husband do not have any children or they are grown children, it may be an older parent or sibling that he should reach out to while he is injured.

Give Him Some Responsibilities

Another way to help your husband to cope at home is to let him take responsibility for some of the light chores around the house and some of the errands that need to be performed. This is especially true if the errands or chores relate to raising the children. This will allow him to feel important by performing very necessary activities which are valuable to you and the family.

He can also help cook meals at home which will give him a feeling of contribution to the family. We understand this may be difficult for you to do as these are the very activities that may define your role in the family. However, we encourage you to relinquish some of these activities to your husband so that he can share in a feeling of responsibility.

There are certain activities that you may want to help your husband avoid which could better help him cope at home. In general, these activities involve spending money. Typically going to the grocery and spending money on the grocery bill can be a very stressful activity following a railroad injury.

He doesn't need to know the tough decisions you are making to make ends meet. The same applies to holiday shopping and birthday shopping. We encourage our clients to think more in terms of "events" and family time during holidays and birthdays rather than material items.

COPING AT HOME
Ways To Help Your Spouse Readjust

Give Him Small Responsibilities

Let him take responsibility for some of the light chores & errands around the house. This will allow him to contribute & help out.

Help Him Appreciate Time With Family

His injury will allow him to spend time with you & his family; you should be aware of this & encourage him to become more involved in your lives now that he is able to do so.

Expand His Social Circle

Helping your husband associate with friends who do not work on the railroad can often help him cope with his injury.

Seek Guidance And/Or Support

It may be helpful to seek spiritual counselling with a preacher, minister or local priest, or find a support group who knows what you're going through.

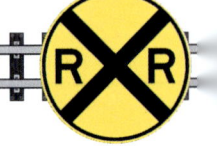

Help Him Associate with Non-Railroad Friends

Helping your husband associate with friends who do not work on the railroad can often help him cope following his injury. Railroad workers tend to be a fraternity of workers who act and think the same way.

It is often difficult for an injured worker to associate with his former coworkers since they will tend to discuss work activities even when they are at home. If your husband has filed a formal claim against the railroad, he absolutely should not associate with former coworkers to any significant degree since this could jeopardize his claim.

Help Him Find Spiritual/Religious Guidance

Finally, it may be helpful for you and your husband to seek spiritual counseling with a preacher, minister or local priest. We do not presume to know whether you, your husband and/or your family are religious, but if so, often it can help by seeking spiritual guidance from your local church.

Life After Filing a Claim

Assuming your husband decides to file an on-duty injury claim against the railroad and his claim is successfully resolved, we offer two closing suggestions which we recommend to all of our clients at the time of their settlements.

Use Settlement Money Wisely

First, use the settlement money wisely for your future. If your husband has had a successful resolution of his claim and it involved a fairly serious claim, you and he may be receiving more cash at this time than you will ever receive at any single time in your future.

It is important to steward the money wisely. It may be meant to last years, not months, and it should be used accordingly.

Living Without Regret and What-Ifs

Additionally, we advise all clients to move on with their lives and not to look back on their previous occupation or the company that they worked for and filed the claim against.

It is natural as adults to think 'what if'. We always want to know what would have happened if we had done something differently. We tend to dwell on the past too much. But often our children can teach us to live in the present and not focus on "what ifs".

We encourage you and your husband to never think 'what if' as you try to move past his injury. Often ours is not to judge why something happened, it is to simply handle it the best way we can with the support of those around us.

This is the final advice we give to our clients in helping them focus on their future and move past a very bad event and time in their lives.

About Us & Our Law Firm, POOLSON | ODEN

We founded the POOLSON | ODEN Law Firm to put the needs of our clients first. It is our privilege to help injured railroaders.

Our goal is to lead our clients from difficult situations to successful outcomes, so that they can move forward with their lives.

It is discouraging whenever we know that the railroad is trying to take advantage of an honest, hard-working worker who has had a serious injury through no fault of his own.

Most often there is an employer/employee relationship, and to us that makes it all the worse when an employer is twisting the laws or facts to get out of paying what it should for the serious damages it caused to one of its own employees.

Most railroaders would prefer not to file a suit. They would rather go on with their careers and turn back the clock to before the accident. We understand that. But hoping to change the past won't make the future any better.

What we do is not simply gather evidence and experts to prove our client's claim in court. That's just the 'legal' part of it. We also counsel our clients on their options and how to map out the best future they can have with the cards they were dealt. We cannot think of a more important service we offer.

We often tell juries in closing arguments that they have a rare opportunity to help a fellow citizen and directly impact a person's life for the better. We tell them they should not waste that chance. We also feel we have that same opportunity with each new client we team up with.

We hope you found this book both helpful and encouraging during your current difficulties. Please phone us if you need anything or have any concerns you want to talk about.

Sincerely,

Danny Poolson & Carisa Oden
POOLSON | ODEN Law Firm

DISCLAIMER:

This book is meant for informational purposes only. The legal statutes mentioned in this book were current as of the publication date, however, we cannot guarantee that these statutes have remained the same since the publication date. The information contained herein is not intended, and should not be taken, as legal advice. You are advised to contact a railroad attorney for counsel on particular issues and concerns. Additionally, your use or request of our materials does not constitute as an attorney-client relationship between you and POOLSON | ODEN Law Firm.

POOLSON | ODEN
RAILROAD INJURY ATTORNEYS

One Lakeway
3900 N. Causeway Blvd.
Suite 680
Metairie, LA 70002
(504) 766-2200 | Office
(833) 505-2122 | Toll Free

WWW.POOLSONODEN.COM

Made in the USA
Middletown, DE
18 September 2023